Series C
Lent • Easter • Ascension • Pentecost

Leaders Guide

By Arthur D. Bacon and
Stephen E. Gaulke

Edited by Thomas J. Doyle

Assistant to the editor: Cindi Crismon

Write to Library for the Blind, 1333 S. Kirkwood Road, St. Louis, Mo 63122-7295 to obtain this study in braille or in large print for the visually impaired.

Scripture quotations are taken from the HOLY BIBLE, NEW INTERNATIONAL VERSION® Copyright © 1973, 1978, 1984 by the International Bible Society. Used by permission of Zondervan Publishing House. All rights reserved.

The "NIV" and "New International Version" trademarks are registered in the United States Patent and Trademark Office by the International Bible Society. Use of either trademark requires the permission of the International Bible Society.

Copyright © 1994 Concordia Publishing House
3558 South Jefferson Avenue, St. Louis, MO 63118-3968
Manufactured in the United States of America

All rights reserved. No part of this publication may be reproduced, stored in a retrieval system, or transmitted, in any form or by any means, electronic, mechanical, photocopying, recording, or otherwise, without the prior written permission of Concordia Publishing House.

Contents

Introduction	4
Session 1: First Sunday in Lent	
Needs: Needed or Needy	5
Session 2: Second Sunday in Lent	
The Master Plan	9
Session 3: Third Sunday in Lent	
Excuse Me	13
Session 4: Fourth Sunday in Lent	
But Now I'm Found	17
Session 5: Fifth Sunday in Lent	
Damned if You Do ... Delivered if You Don't	21
Session 6: Palm Sunday (Sunday of the Passion)	
The Day in the Life of Jesus	25
Session 7: Maundy Thursday	
The Best Meal You Ever Had	29
Session 8: Good Friday	
The Worst Suffering, the Best Result	33
Session 9: The Resurrection of Our Lord	
He Won the Victory and So Did We	36
Session 10: Second Sunday of Easter	
Surprise, Surprise, Surprise	39
Session 11: Third Sunday of Easter	
Once Was Blind but Now I See	43
Session 12: Fourth Sunday of Easter	
The Lamb Is the Shepherd	46
Session 13: Fifth Sunday of Easter	
What's New about Love?	49
Session 14: Sixth Sunday of Easter	
Departures and Arrivals	52
Session 15: The Ascension of Our Lord	
I Told You So!	55
Session 16: Seventh Sunday of Easter	
Behind Closed Doors	59
Session 17: The Festival of Pentecost	
Gathering to Scatter	62

Introduction

About the Series

This course is 1 of 12 in the Church Year series. The Bible studies in this series are tied to the 3-year lectionary. These studies give participants the opportunity to explore the Old Testament lesson (or lesson from the book of Acts during the Easter season), the Epistle lesson, and the Gospel lesson appointed for each Sunday of the church year. Also, optional studies give participants the opportunity to study in depth the lessons appointed for festival days during the church year that fall on days other than Sunday (e.g., Ascension Day, Reformation, Christmas Day, Christmas Eve, Maundy Thursday, Good Friday, Epiphany).

Book 1 for years A, B, and C in the lectionary series will include 17 studies of the Scripture lessons appointed for the Sundays and festival days in Advent, Christmas, and Epiphany. Book 2 will include 17 studies of the lessons appointed for the Sundays and festival days in Lent and Easter and of lessons appointed for Ascension and Pentecost. Book 3 (15 sessions) and 4 (16 sessions) for years A, B, and C include studies that focus on the lessons appointed for the Pentecost season.

After a brief review and textual study of the Scripture lessons appointed for a Sunday or festival day, each study is designed to help participants draw conclusions about each of the lessons, compare and contrast the lessons, discover a unifying theme in the lessons (if possible), and apply the theme to their lives. At the end of each study, the Scripture lessons for the next Sunday and/or festival day are assigned for participants to read in preparation for the next study. The leaders guide for each course provides additional textual information on appointed lessons, answers to the questions in the study guide, a suggested process for teaching the study, and devotional or worship activities tied to the theme.

May the Holy Spirit richly bless you as you study God's Word!

Session 1

First Sunday in Lent

Deuteronomy 26:5–10; Romans 10:8b–13; Luke 4:1–13

Focus

Theme: *Needs: Needed or Needy*

Law/Gospel Focus

Read aloud the Law/Gospel statement. Have participants identify the Law in the first three sentences and the Gospel in the final statement.

Objectives

Read aloud or have a volunteer read aloud the objectives.

Opening Worship

Pray together the responsive prayer.

Introduction

Encourage the participants to discuss the questions either in the large group or in smaller groups.
1. Responses will vary.
2. Responses will vary.
3. God provides us His Gospel, "This Son I give to you who will meet your greatest need!"

Inform

If the participants have not read the lessons before the class session, it may be necessary to read the lessons aloud at this time. A brief summary of the lessons is provided in the study guide to help focus attention on the important messages of the texts.

The Old Testament lesson is Deut. 26:5–10. Deuteronomy means "second law." The book records Moses' farewell sermons. As the wilderness wanderings end, Moses knows God's people are about to enter promised Palestine without him. So he "seconds" the "law" God had given His people from Mount Sinai almost four decades earlier. The people dare not forget God's love as they now go into the good land. Before class, read Deut. 26:1–11 for the context of Moses' words.

The Epistle lesson is Rom. 10:8b–13. Paul tells of our heart's need and of our mouth's creed. We respond to God's love for us in Christ with thankful hearts and mouths that confess boldly His love to others.

The Gospel lesson, Luke 4:1–13, is discussed in the next four questions.

Have the participants work individually or in small groups to discuss the questions that follow the summaries.

1. Man does live on bread, but only the bread that God gives. How much more bread, more money, more material "stuff" do we need? Satan desires to make the bread (things) of this world our god. God promises to give us the bread we need. Not one crumb too much or too little, He gives what is best!

2. We are most needy for the love and forgiveness only Jesus can provide. After God took care of our neediness through His Son's death and resurrection, He provided us with opportunities to serve Him—to proclaim His love to others who remain needy in their sins.

    You may ask participants to consider Mark 10:45, "The Son of Man did not come to be served, but to serve, and to give His life as a ransom for many." Jesus' service has taken away the sins of all the world, and mine! As the Holy Spirit enables us to respond to God's goodness in lives of service to Him, He also works in us to serve others as part of that response.

3. Do not put the Lord your God to the test! We may feel special feelings. The world may see spectacular wonders. But neither feelings nor spectacular wonders prove God. Ask participants, "By what one wonderful sign did God show His love for us?" Read Phil. 2:8. "Christ Jesus humbled Himself and became obedient to death—even death on a cross." What proof, what spectacle, has He promised still to come? Read Phil. 2:9–11. "Therefore God exalted Him to the highest place and gave Him the name that is

above every name, that at the name of Jesus every knee should bow, in heaven and on earth and under the earth, and every tongue confess that Jesus Christ is Lord, to the glory of God the Father." Today, God empowers us through His Word and sacraments, giving us forgiveness, the strength to resist temptation, and the desire and ability to proclaim His love to others.
4. Jesus had to defeat the devil as a man so that His victory could substitute for our defeat. He triumphed as the true Son of Man.

Connect

1. Deut. 26:5 remembers the "wandering Aramean's" need for
   (a) the promised homeland, and for
   (b) the promised multiplication of his "few people." God did bring Jacob/Israel out of exile from Aram/Syria to promised Palestine. But there he fathered only one small nomad tribe among the many landed natives (Gen. 27–35). God made the next generations the promised "great nation, powerful and numerous."
   (c) Ask, "What is our promised homeland?" The Apostles' Creed anticipates our heavenly "life everlasting," and the Nicene "the life of the world to come," where Jesus' "kingdom will have no end."
2. (a) Deut. 26:6–8 recalls how Israel's children, under "misery, toil, and oppression," needed freedom from Egypt's "hard labor."
   (b) God answered when He told Moses, "Raise your (shepherd's) staff and stretch out your hand" (see Ex. 7:19–20; 14:16–27). "With great terror and with miraculous signs and wonders," God freed Moses' generation.
   (c) Ask, "What has God done about our 'hard labor' under sin's slavery?" God's "mighty hands" (nail-pierced) and "outstretched arms" (crucified) are remembered in the Apostles' Creed as He "suffered under Pontius Pilate, was crucified, died and was buried." The Nicene recalls that Jesus "was crucified also for us under Pontius Pilate." The Apostles' Creed celebrates "the forgiveness of sins." The Nicene even names our "Red Sea crossing"—"I acknowledge one Baptism for the remission of sins."
3. (a) Deut. 26:9 retells the next generation's need to be "brought to this place."
   (b) So God "gave us this land, a land flowing with milk and honey."

The fruits of promised Palestine were to feed Israel's every generation.
  (c) Ask, "What will God do for us, so that even physically we may know His care forever?" "I look for the resurrection of the dead," says the Nicene Creed. The Apostles' Creed specifies, "the resurrection of the body."
4. Jesus three times quoted Scripture. "It is written." Say, "In Eph. 6:17, St. Paul urges us, 'Take … the sword of the Spirit, which is the word of God.'" You may investigate further Is. 49:2; Heb. 4:12; Rev. 1:16; 2:12,16. Rom. 10:8–9 says that sword "is near you." For God's Word—Holy Scripture—is professed by our "mouth" and believed in our "heart."
5. Ask a volunteer to find and read aloud Matt. 1:21. Here the angel tells Joseph, "She will give birth to a son, and you are to give Him the name Jesus, because He will save His people from their sins." "Jesus" is Hebrew for "Yahweh saves," "the LORD rescues." Have the participants share needs for which Jesus has provided. God's Word is Jesus. "The Word was God.… The Word became flesh and made His dwelling among us" (John 1:1,14; or see Heb. 1:1–2).

Vision

During This Week

Discuss these activities with the participants. Suggest, "Pick a partner to whom you will report your experience with one of these activities before we gather again next week."

Closing Worship

Pray together the responsive prayer.

Scripture Lessons for Next Sunday

Assign the appointed lessons for the Second Sunday in Lent.

Session 2

Second Sunday in Lent

Jeremiah 26:8–15; Philippians 3:17–4:1; Luke 13:31–35

Focus

Theme: *The Master Plan*

Law/Gospel Focus

Read aloud the Law/Gospel statement. Have participants identify the Law statement in the first sentence and the Gospel statement in the second.

Objectives

Read aloud or have a volunteer read aloud the objectives.

Opening Worship

Pray together the responsive prayer.

Introduction

Read aloud the opening question. Answers will vary.

Inform

If the participants have not read the lessons before the class session, it may be necessary to read the lessons aloud at this time. A brief summary of the lessons is provided in the study guide to help focus attention on the important messages of the texts.

Jer. 26:8–15—Is the context of this text unfamiliar? Read some brief introduction to Jeremiah, such as that provided in the *Concordia Self-Study Bible*, for an overview of Jeremiah's times, life, and prophecies. For your personal preparation, read all of Jer. 26.

From the days of Joshua's conquest (1,400 B.C.), Shiloh had been the town of God's holy Tabernacle tent. Then David's kingdom (1,000

B.C.) moved the Ark of the Covenant to Jerusalem, the city of God's holy temple. In 930 B.C., David's grandson reigned over the split of the kingdom. In 722 B.C., 100 years before Jeremiah, the Assyrian Empire demolished the northern kingdom of Israel (with Shiloh). Assyria then put the kingdom of Judah (southern Israel, with Jerusalem) under her boot.

Now in 612 B.C., Assyria was toppled by Babylon (today's Iraq). So the priests and false prophets hatched their pious plots to free God's people. Yet they had no regard for the Lord's plan! They looked not to the Lord for rescue, but to Egypt. In 605 B.C., Nebuchadnezzar's Babylonians crushed the Pharaoh's Egyptian army. In 586 B.C., just as Jeremiah had prophesied, Nebuchadnezzar leveled the Lord's temple "like Shiloh," enslaved Judah's royal house, and left the capital city Jerusalem "desolate and deserted."

Phil. 3:17–4:1—In his teaching, Paul unmasks the plots of both labored legalists and licentious libertines. The legalists falsely teach, "God's Law enslaves you to save yourself." The self-righteous would work to death! The libertines falsely teach, "God's Gospel frees you to serve yourself." The self-serving would sin to death!

In his conduct, Paul's example echoes Christ's plan. Only Jesus' righteousness, only His serving, frees us to life. Only the Crucified's deathstyle leads to the resurrection lifestyle. (See Phil. 1:12–14; 3:7–11.)

Luke 13:31–35—Herod already had taken John the Baptizer's head, and was perplexed over Jesus (Luke 3:19–20; 9:7–9). Whether these Pharisees were genuinely friendly towards Jesus (they were no friends of impious Herod) or only hypocritically plotting (Jesus sends them back to "that fox"), matters not. "Today and tomorrow and the next day" Jesus will do that which fulfills God's plan. He will "keep going" until the big day. "And on the third day I will reach My goal" (compare Luke 9:22; 18:33; 24:7, 46).

1. We will see, in question 3 below, that even those who plotted Christ's death believed they were "doing this for God" (Matt. 26:59–66).
2. Rom. 8:28 may speak to your discussion. "In all things God works for the good of those who love Him, who have been called according to His purpose." But God has not promised that we will always recognize what that good was, not on this side of eternity.
3. The Scriptures repeatedly assert that Jesus fulfills the promise of Israel's "house." For example, in Matt. 12:6, Jesus claims He is Jerusalem's true "house." "I tell you that one greater than the tem-

ple is here." God's plan hinged on His Son being destroyed and in three days raised again.

Those who plotted Jesus' death did not "get it." Jesus said, "You (unbelievers) destroy this temple" (John 2:19). Three years later they twisted His words to, "This fellow said, 'I (Jesus) am able to destroy the temple'" (Matt. 26:61). So they plotted the destruction of His holy body.

4. God punished the innocent One for the sins of the world. The Father, withholding His heavenly love, poured out hell's fury on His Son. The Father abandoned His sinless Son, that He may forever embrace His Son's sinful brothers and sisters. See also Gal. 3:13. Because Jesus was our substitute, we shall never be desolate, deserted, nor damned.

5. Jerusalem on Palm Sunday actually saw Jesus with their eyes, but did not fully, faithfully grasp whom they were praising. We, the "new Jerusalem," in these post-Easter, pre-Second Coming days, see Jesus with eyes of faith, and do "bless Him who comes." Old (unbelieving) Jerusalem and new (faithful) Jerusalem both will actually see Jesus on the Last Day, and every tongue will bless and confess His name.

6. We joyfully bless the Lord, taking to heart His happy blessing when we worship! We are not desolate, for Jesus comes to us in His Word and in His sacraments. He graced us with His long-planned rescue!

Connect

1. Jesus reached His goal on Easter (Luke 13:32), proclaiming new life for all the world. His goal has been accomplished in us, gathered into His holy (Baptized clean) community of (forgiven sinner) saints.

   But others are still "not willing" (Luke 13:34). "Many live as enemies of the cross of Christ" (Phil. 3:18). To these people Jesus gives all the time in the world. Little time is left! He promised, "And this gospel of the kingdom will be preached in the whole world as a testimony to all nations, and then the end will come" (Matt. 24:14).

   You, and your church, fit into the Master's plan as by your words and actions He gathers still more of those for whom Jesus died and rose.

2. "Our citizenship is in heaven" now. Our "life everlasting" began when our Baptism (see Rom. 6:4) joined us to Jesus' resurrection. We are aliens. Christ won our citizenship in heaven on the cross.
3. Responses will vary.
4. Our lowly bodies will be transformed like Jesus' glorious body. Paul discusses our risen body most thoroughly in 1 Cor. 15:35–58. He describes our resurrected body as imperishable, glorious, powerful, spiritual, and immortal. You may consider some wonderful attributes of Jesus' risen body in the Easter accounts. The risen Christ is recognizable and touchable (Matt. 28:9; Luke 24:39; John 20:17, 20, 27). He even eats (Luke 24:43). But His body is not bound by space (Luke 24:31, 36, 51; John 20:19, 26).
5. Jesus "longed to gather your children together, as a hen gathers her chicks" (Luke 13:34). "For the joy set before Him," so pleased to ransom us, He "endured the cross" (Heb. 12:2). Jesus grieves that "you were not willing" to be gathered under His wing. Later, on Palm Sunday, "as He approached Jerusalem and saw the city, He wept over it" (Luke 19:41).

    Paul must "now say again even with tears, many live as enemies of the cross of Christ." Still, joyfully, "we eagerly await a Savior." On the Last Day the Lord Jesus Christ will finally, fully deliver us from all evil.

    We should weep for those who reject Christ, as we were born rejecting Him ourselves. We testify to Jesus' resurrection as we rejoice that He lives to gather all people, as He has us, under His saving wing.

Vision

During This Week

Discuss these activities with the participants. Urge them to complete at least one during the week.

Closing Worship

Read together the responsive prayer.

Scripture Lessons for Next Sunday

Assign the appointed lessons for the Third Sunday in Lent.

Session 3

Third Sunday in Lent

Exodus 3:1–8a, 10–15; 1 Corinthians 10:1–13; Luke 13:1–9

> ## Focus
>
> **Theme:** *Excuse Me*
>
> **Law/Gospel Focus**
> Read aloud the Law/Gospel statement.
>
> **Objectives**
> Read aloud or have a volunteer read aloud the objectives.
>
> **Opening Worship**
> Lead the responsive prayer.

Introduction

Read aloud the opening paragraphs. Discuss the questions that follow either in small groups or with the entire class. Responses will vary.

Inform

If the participants have not read the lessons before the class sessions, it may be necessary to read the lessons aloud at this time. A brief summary of the lessons is provided in the study guide to help focus attention on the important messages of the texts.

Ex. 3:1–8a, 10–15—For your own preparation, read the background of this text in Ex. 2 (as well as the Epistle lesson) and Acts 7:20–44.

1 Cor. 10:1–13—Explore Paul's Old Testament references. Israel's "baptism;" Ex. 13:21; 14:22, 29. Israel's communion; Ex. 16:4–15;

17:6; Num. 20:11. Only Caleb and Joshua enter the promised land; Num. 14:29–30. Idolatry; Ex. 32:4–6. Sexual immorality; Num. 25:1–9. Testing the Lord; Num. 21:5–6.Grumbling; Num. 16:41–49.

Paul would not have us abandon the sacraments for fear of using them faithlessly. Rather use these means of grace, these funnels of God's undeserved love, faithfully. By their Gospel power alone can we stand tall! The questions in "Connect" will offer further opportunity to discuss this.

Luke 13:1–9—The accounts of the Galileans slaughtered and the Siloam tower tragedy are not otherwise told in Scripture, nor in the secular histories. Jesus himself grew up in Nazareth, and now resided in Capernaum, both in Galilee (northern Israel). Devout Galileans came south to Jerusalem's temple to offer their sacrifices. Note that the Holy City herself suffered this world's tragedies.

1. Jesus tells us twice, with emphasis, "Unless you repent, you too will all perish" (Luke 13:3, 5). Trouble certainly is a result of sin, but God sent His Son to experience the punishment we deserved because of His displeasure over our sins.
2. The confession of sins is in full harmony with Jesus' clear Law. "O almighty God … I have ever offended You and justly deserved Your punishment now and forever."

    God has mercy, putting the punishment due the world's sin on the crucified Jesus. Millions do "repent," believing that for all sinners Jesus Himself suffered death and hell. "Whoever believes in Him shall not perish but have eternal life" (John 3:16).
3. Jesus would have us turn from sin, towards Him who saves from sin. True repentance always involves both grief and trust. "Repentant believers are those who are sorry for their sins (contrition) and who believe in the Lord Jesus Christ as their Savior (faith)."

    In the worship service participants repent in the confession ("I am heartily sorry") and confess faith in the creed ("I believe"). You can see both parts also in the Kyrie ("Lord, have mercy") and the Gloria ("Glory to God in the highest, and peace to His people on earth").
4. Christ's forgiveness changes our whole relationship to God, to ourselves, and to our neighbor. We can admit "I am sorry," and trust, "God has forgiven me." God's forgiveness motivates us to forgive when we have been sinned against, and also to speak God's forgiveness to all.

Connect

1. This question is the "flip side" of Inform, question 1. Thank the Lord for His every kindness towards us. But trust not in those kindnesses! To those who live faithlessly, the triumphs of this life guarantee nothing more than God's giving that "one more year" to bear the fruit of repentance. Those without excuse He finally does chop down.
2. "In all things God works for the good of those who love him" (Rom. 8:28). God has promised to work in us His life-giving forgiveness through His Word and through His sacraments. Nothing less than these means can nurture our spiritual fruitfulness.
3. God's displeasure with old Israel, as with us (new Israel), runs deeper than their sins. These sins betrayed their belief in self-deification. "Lord, do this my way. In us we trust!"
4. Israel failed with their gifts. They set their hearts, not on God's promises, but "on evil things" (1 Cor. 10:6). "God is faithful" (1 Cor. 10:13). But Israel fell for the temptations at hand, rather than trusting their Lord.
5. Believe, trust, have faith in God's clear promise! The Lord, as the Catechism makes clear, will not excuse the faithless use of Christ's sacraments. Not simple sins, but the rejection of Jesus with His forgiveness, finally dooms those damned.
6. Romans 6:4—"We were therefore buried with Him through baptism into death in order that, just as Christ was raised from death through the glory of the Father, we too may live a new life." In the Small Catechism Luther comments on this passage as he pictures Baptism's power for the Christian's life. Baptism "indicates that the Old Adam in us should by daily contrition and repentance be drowned and die with all sins and evil desires, and that a new man should daily emerge and arise to live before God in righteousness and purity forever."

    1 Cor. 11:26—"For whenever you eat this bread and drink this cup, you proclaim the Lord's death until He comes." Our communing proclaims to our world that our community (congregation—Paul's "you" is plural in Greek) lives by communion (unity) with the risen Lord who died for our forgiveness. Our communing proclaims that the divine Savior, who now comes to us with His human body and blood for our forgiveness, will next come as divine Judge to bring us to His Holy Feast above.

Point out that the Old Testament sacrificial system pointed to the once for all sacrifice of Christ. As we remember Christ's sacrifice in the sacrament of the Altar, we also receive its benefits of forgiveness, salvation, and renewed spiritual strength.
7. We have no excuse, because "God is faithful; He will not let you be tempted beyond what you can bear."

As they give to us Christ's forgiveness for fruitless living, the Holy Spirit works through the sacraments to strengthen our faith. Strengthening our faith, the sacraments also give us Christ's power for fruitful living. Given His power, we can stand firm under temptation.

Vision

During This Week

Discuss these activities with the participants. Encourage them to complete at least one during the week.

Closing Worship

Lead the responsive prayer.

Scripture Lessons for Next Sunday

Assign the appointed lessons for the Fourth Sunday in Lent.

Session 4

Fourth Sunday in Lent

Isaiah 12:1–6; 1 Corinthians 1:18–31; Luke 15:1–3, 11–32

Focus

Theme: *But Now I'm Found*

Law/Gospel Focus

Read aloud the Law/Gospel statement. Ask participants to circle the subject of the first clause ("I"), and underline the subject of the second Gospel clause ("Father").

Objectives

Read aloud or have a volunteer read aloud the objectives.

Opening Worship

Sing or pray together the first and third stanzas of "Amazing Grace."

Introduction

Read aloud the questions. Have participants discuss the questions that follow in small groups. Answers will vary.

Inform

If the participants have not read the lessons before the class session, it may be necessary to read the lessons aloud at this time. A brief summary of the lessons is provided in the study guide to help focus attention on the important messages of the texts.

Is. 12:1–6—"In that day you will say …," twice sings Isaiah (verses 1 and 4). What day? The twin psalms of Is. 12 close his previous section of prophecies (Is. 7–11). "The virgin will be with child and will give birth to a son, and will call Him Immanuel" (7:14). "The people walking in darkness have seen a great light" (9:2). "For to us a child is born" (9:6). "In that day the Root of Jesse will stand as a banner for the peoples … His place of rest will be glorious" (11:10). 700 years before Easter, 2,700 plus years before the final Day of Resurrection, Isaiah rejoices to see the day the Messiah comes to reign! He sings the joy of the prodigal son restored to his Father's home.

1 Cor. 1:18–31—Paul's theology of the cross is the heartbeat of Christianity. Martin Luther comments, "All works, however holy they may be, are completely excluded and put aside as unnecessary for our salvation. If a good work saves a man, then apples and pears also save him. Christian righteousness is not a righteousness that is within us and clings to us as a quality or virtue does, that is, something that is found to be part of us or something that is felt by us. But it is a foreign righteousness entirely outside us, namely, Christ himself is "our *formalis Iustitia*,' our essential Righteousness and complete Satisfaction" (1 Cor. 1:30). (*What Luther Says* 3916 [vol. III, p.1230], CPH, 1959.)

Luke 15:1–3; 11–32—People treasure this parable for its rich message. As you read Jesus' story again in your preparations, note your favorite part. Why does this part speak to you? Ask God to show you, and the participants also, new gems in these familiar words.

1. The younger son demands, "Give me." His trouble blossoms from his putting "me" and "my share" ahead of his father and his love. Encourage participants to respond to the question.
2. Our Father warns, in His First Commandment, "You shall have no other gods." Our Father promises to welcome and restore us, and so turns our hearts toward Him (repentance). "You, My sons and daughters, were dead. But I make you alive again. You were lost. But I have found you!" "God, who is rich in mercy, made us alive with Christ even when we were dead in transgressions" (Eph. 2:4–5).
3. The elder son accuses, "You never gave me." Like his brother and like you and me, he was a born believer in himself as god.
4. The First Commandment reveals that our failure to love our Father seeds our failure to love our siblings. Our Father pledges Himself to us. "I am with you always" (Matt. 28:20), He says by His one good Son. "Everything I have is yours." The Epistle lesson from the first Sunday in Lent promises, "The same Lord is Lord of all and richly blesses all who call on Him" (Rom. 10:12b).
5. The father looks "foolish" as he restores the son who wasted his

fortune, "weak" as he pleads with the son who boasts in self-righteousness. So Jesus pictures our Father's wisdom in winning sinners, His strength in turning the self-righteous toward home.

Connect

1. Spend about four to five minutes role playing the characters from the prodigal son.
2. The new clothes and high feast make tangible all the love his father has promised by his hug and kiss. These tangibles the son always has at hand and can always show to others.
3. God gives us His Gospel Word and His sacraments. "You are all sons of God through faith in Christ Jesus, for all of you who were baptized into Christ have clothed yourselves with Christ" (Gal. 3:26–27). Note how Paul describes Baptism as God's family robe. "This is My body ... My blood ... for you" (Luke 22:19–20). Note how our Father sacrificed His best, His one good Son. The sacraments make tangible all the love our Father's Word has promised.
4. Isaiah's song fits our mouths as well as the prodigal's mouth. Because of the cross, God's "anger has turned away." Because of Christ, "the Lord is my strength and my song, He has become my salvation."
5. Isaiah's second song reflects a reconciliation with the prodigal's brother. We would "make known among the nations what the Lord has done." We rejoice in our Father's weak and foolish ways. He has restored even the self-righteous!
6. Paul identifies at the heart of God's amazing grace. "We preach Christ crucified" (1 Cor. 1:23). The storyteller gave His life so that His story comes true and ours has a happy ending! Accept participant examples of evidence of God's wisdom and power in their lives.

Vision

During This Week

Encourage participants to complete at least one of these activities during the week.

Closing Worship

This closing worship weaves together key phrases from today's Scripture readings and from Lutheran Worship's Divine Service II. During Lent most congregations do not sing the Hymn of Praise, "This is the Feast of Victory for Our God" (p. 161) nor Post-Communion Canticle "Thank the Lord." We save these joyous "Alleluias" until Easter.

Scripture Lessons for Next Sunday

Assign the appointed lessons for the Fifth Sunday in Lent.

Session 5

Fifth Sunday in Lent

Isaiah 43:16–21; Philippians 3:8–14; Luke 20:9–19

Focus

Theme: *Damned if You Do ... Delivered if You Don't*

Law/Gospel Focus

Read aloud the Law/Gospel statement. Have participants underline once the Law statement in the first sentence and circle the Gospel statement in the second and third sentences.

Objectives

Read aloud or have a volunteer read aloud the objectives.

Opening Worship

Pray together the responsive prayer from Is. 43:16–19.

Introduction

The leader or a volunteer should read aloud the opening paragraph. Discuss the questions in the second paragraph. Return repeatedly to the issues raised from these questions in today's Bible study.

Inform

If the participants have not read the lessons before the class session, it may be necessary to read the lessons aloud at this time. A brief summary of the lessons is provided in the study guide to help focus attention on the important messages of the texts.

Is. 43:16–21—The study guide discusses how Isaiah's words first applied to his contemporary hearers. The opening and closing worship apply Isaiah's words to us.

Phil. 3:8–14—In your personal preparations and for the context of Paul's words read Phil. 3. The Epistle readings, also for the Second Sunday in Lent and Palm/Passion Sunday, come from this letter. The missionary writes his letter to the Philippians while "in chains for Christ" (1:13). For this imprisoned present and his heavenly future, he has rejected his Christless past as "rubbish."

Luke 20:9–19—This parable is recorded also in Matt. 21:33–46 and Mark 12:1–12, with different details. Mark 11:1–12, 19–20, 27; and 13:1 makes plain that Jesus is teaching in the temple on the Tuesday after Palm Sunday, three days before Good Friday.

Have the participants work individually or in small groups to discuss the questions that follow the summaries.

1. List the players on the chalkboard or on sheets of newsprint.

    The owner is God.

    The vineyard is Israel. Jesus builds His parable on one well known to His hearers, Is. 5:1–7. Remember also Luke 13:6 from two Sundays ago. "A man had a fig tree, planted in his vineyard, and he went to look for fruit on it."

    The tenants are Israel's leaders. See verse 19.

    The fruit are good deeds done in loving faith. Compare to the baptizer's "fruits of repentance" (Luke 3:8–9).

    The servants are the prophets. Remember Luke 13:34, from three weeks back. "O Jerusalem, Jerusalem, you who kill the prophets and stone those sent to you, how often I have longed to gather your children together."

    The Son is Jesus. Compare God's affirmation at Jesus' Baptism, "You are My Son, whom I love; with You I am well pleased" (Luke 3:22) and the Transfiguration, "This is My Son, whom I have chosen; listen to Him" (Luke 9:35).

    The others are those in the church. Matt. 21:43 appends Jesus' explanation to this parable. "The kingdom of God will be taken away from you and given to a people who will produce its fruit." Christ's church is the "new Israel," composed of the people from old Israel and from all nations who believe in Him.

2. "The love of money is a root of all kinds of evil," says Paul (1 Tim. 6:10). Our grasping greed is seeded in our desire to serve self, rather than God. Recall, from your discussion on the third Sunday in Lent, that faithlessness produces fruitlessness. But none can quiet God's message by killing His messengers.

3. Paul trusts Christ. He treasures the Giver of the gifts.
4. In Lent, we sing, "Return to the Lord, your God, for He is gracious and merciful, slow to anger, and abounding in steadfast love, and abounding in steadfast love" (*LW* p. 165). "God so loved the world" (John 3:16). "Love is patient, love is kind … It is not easily angered, it keeps no record of wrongs" (1 Cor. 13:4–6).
5. "God so loved the world that He gave His one and only Son, that whoever believes in Him shall not perish" (John 3:16). "The cross is foolishness to those who are perishing," said Paul (1 Cor. 1:18).
6. Sin would lead us to deny or disregard God. In a sense, sin leads us to proclaim, "God is dead." My sin did crucify Christ!

Connect

1. The father's sending three servants and his son shows the Father's endless desire to forgive wicked deeds. But those who reject the Father's forgiveness are damned. Jesus is "the stone the builders rejected." Jesus summarizes God's Law. "Do not reject the Father's Son, or He will damn you!"
2. Paul confesses, "not having a righteousness of my own that comes from the law." But he stands right with God "through faith in Christ—the righteousness that comes from God and is by faith." Faith grasps the mercy won for all the world by Christ's self-sacrifice. Paul summarizes the Gospel, "Do receive the Father's Son, for He has delivered you!"
3. Both those who reject and ignore Jesus are "broken to pieces" and "crushed."

    In the verse before our Epistle, Paul recalls his former "zeal in persecuting the church." The resurrected "capstone" smashed the old life of Paul, just as it smashes the old life of all who come to faith in Christ Jesus.
4. Jesus could, in silence, let the chief priests and teachers of the law go to hell. He speaks, hoping they will repent so He might deliver them. Perhaps if not now, then after His sacrifice some may see their sin and turn to Him as Savior. Jesus' parable makes plain that the Son deliberately goes to His death, for this death is His Father's desire. His warning words will further reveal His righteousness.

5. Luke records two unique Gospel words from Christ's cross. "Father, forgive them, for they do not know what they are doing" (23:34). "I tell you the truth, today you will be with Me in paradise" (23:43). Beside His faith-creating promise, Jesus left His own faithful example. "Father, into Your hands I commit My spirit" (23:46).
6. God's forgiveness for us in Christ moves us to be forgiving toward others.

Vision

During This Week

Discuss these activities with the participants. Encourage them to complete at least one during the week.

Closing Worship

Pray together the responsive prayer from Ps. 103:8–17a.

Scripture Lessons for Next Sunday

Assign the appointed lessons for Palm Sunday.

Session 6

Palm Sunday (Sunday of the Passion)

Deuteronomy 32:36–39; Philippians 2:5–11; Luke 22:1–23:56

Focus

Theme: *The Day in the Life of Jesus*

Law/Gospel Focus

Read aloud the Law/Gospel statement. Have participants underline once the Law statement in the first sentence and circle the Gospel statement in the second sentence.

Objectives

Ask a volunteer to read aloud the objectives.

Opening Worship

Pray together the responsive litany.

Introduction

Explain to participants that this lesson focuses primarily on the last day in the life of Jesus. Allow participants to respond individually to the questions. Then allow volunteers to share their responses. Do not force anyone to share. Responses will vary.

Inform

If the participants have not read the lessons before the class session, it may be necessary to read the lessons aloud at this time. A brief summary of the lessons is provided in the study guide to help focus attention on the important messages of the texts.

The Old Testament lesson, Deut. 32:36–39, focuses on the relationship between Israel and the Lord. God will judge, but this reading emphasizes God's compassion for His people. Only when they recognize their helplessness will God then intervene redemptively for them in the midst of their godly sorrow.

The Epistle lesson, Phil. 2:5–11, shows the humility of Jesus who in His pre-incarnate state was God and yet, willingly humbled Himself and became man. He did this in order to save us by becoming the suffering servant. Jesus put aside all personal rights and interests so that our eternal welfare might be insured. As a consequence, God exalted Him and states that universal recognition will be His one day. All will confess "Jesus Christ is Lord" on the final day.

The Gospel lesson, Luke 22:1–23:56, is the final chapter in *the day* of Jesus' death. The topics of the reading begin with the Last Supper where Judas' heinous betrayal occurs and our Lord institutes His Holy Meal. After Jesus prays in the garden, He is arrested and taken before the high priests, while Peter denies his association with Jesus. Pilate condemns our innocent Lord to the cross where Jesus dies. *The day* of Jesus' death ends with Jesus being buried. All appears to be tragically lost at this point.

Have the participants work individually or in small groups to discuss the questions.

1. God has the right to judge His people who have strayed far from Him. God has the right to show compassion toward His people. Nevertheless, God's gracious actions on behalf of a people who deserve condemnation are nothing short of divine love.
2. While we deserve only God's wrath and condemnation for our rebellion, God in His great love, heals, brings to life, and delivers His people.
    Ps. 34:18—God remains close to us in the valleys of life, assuring us of His salvation.
    Eph. 2:8–9—God saves us by His grace through faith in Jesus, not by our actions.
    Titus 3:5—God saves us through Holy Baptism.
3. Paul urges us to demonstrate an attitude of humility and servanthood.
4. We pay homage to Jesus as we confess Him as Lord. In this way we bring glory to God our Father in heaven.
5. Answers will vary. Possible answers might include the following information.

The Last Supper—We celebrate as we receive the gifts of forgiveness and eternal life given in His body and blood as we recall His death and resurrection on our behalf.

Jesus in the Garden—Our Lord prayed to His heavenly Father in the midst of events which He knew were about to culminate in His death.

Jesus' Trial—The innocent Lord received an unjust trial which resulted in an unjust judgment. The just man faces the injustice of the high priests and the Roman governor.

The Crucifixion—The greatest moment in all of history occurs when tragic events culminate on the tree of death, yet ironically for us that same tree is the tree of life. He paid for our sins on that tree. The words to the thief on the cross are words we can also cling to—"Today you will be with Me in paradise."

The Burial—What appears as the saddest moment in all of history occurs when the body of our Lord is placed in the tomb. His body was claimed by a "silent" follower, Joseph, and wrapped in linen.

Connect

Ask a volunteer to read the opening paragraph and then have the participants work in small groups to discuss the questions.

1. Is. 53:4—This is the day when Jesus took the punishment for our sin upon Himself as He was stricken, smitten, and afflicted.

    1 Cor. 15:3—This is the day when Christ died for your sins, thereby fulfilling God's promise of a Savior for His world.

    Gal. 1:4—Jesus fulfilled the Father's will on this day in order to rescue you from this evil age.

    Heb. 9:28—The once and for all sacrifice was made on this day for the sins of the world (your sins). His return signals that heaven awaits those who believe in Him.

    Rev. 5:9—Jesus, the Lamb, was slain on this day in order to win salvation for all people, including you.

2. Responses to both questions may vary.

    a. They might include honoring God with our first fruits, kneeling in prayer, obeying the Lord, and standing firm on the truth as taught in God's Word.

    b. We can confess Jesus to our children, family, and guests in our

home through our words as well as through our actions. We confess Jesus by our actions, and by our words of love and forgiveness on the job. We confess Jesus to our friends through our loving relationships and by our words.
3. In our Baptism we participate in His death and resurrection. In Him we bury sin and rise to new life. The old ways of sinful living no longer control us as Christ empowers us to turn to God and live in obedience to His will. In Christ, each day provides new opportunities for humble service to Him.

Vision

During This Week
Discuss these activities with the participants. Urge them to complete at least one during the week.

Closing Worship
Sing or pray together "Take My Life, O Lord, Renew" (*LW 404*).

Scripture Lessons for Maunday Thursday
Assign the appointed lessons for Maundy Thursday.

Session 7

Maundy Thursday

Jeremiah 31:31–34; Hebrews 10:15–39; Luke 22:7–20

Focus

Theme: *The Best Meal You Ever Had*

Law/Gospel Focus:

Read aloud the Law/Gospel statement. Have participants underline once the Law statement in the first sentence and circle the Gospel statement in the second and third sentences.

Objectives

Read aloud or have a volunteer read aloud the objectives.

Opening Worship

Pray together the litany.

Introduction

Have participants work independently. Then provide time for participants to share their answers.

Inform

If the participants have not read the lessons before the class session, it may be necessary to read the lessons aloud at this time. A brief summary of the lessons is provided in the study guide to help focus attention on the important messages of the texts.

The Old Testament lesson, Jer. 31:31–34, predicts the coming of God's Savior. The new covenant, established by God, means not more laws, but rather a new heart for people. He provides a new motivation for obeying His will. The center of the new covenant is the free gift of forgiveness of sins that God offers to people everywhere.

The Epistle lesson, Heb. 10:15–39, speaks of the results of the new covenant God graciously provides His people—we can "draw near with a true heart," we can be sure of our forgiveness, we can spur one another to good works, we can encourage one another. Such is not a result for those who continue to sin. The writer of Hebrews encourages us to cling in confidence to the Lord amid all your trials. Jesus' promise to return is true and certain.

The Gospel lesson, Luke 22:7–20, speaks of Jesus instituting a new covenant for His people. In the midst of the solemn Old Testament Passover meal the Lord establishes the celebration where He assures us of the forgiveness of our sins through His body and blood.

Have the participants discuss the questions in small groups.

1. The term "covenant" in Scripture involves God's gracious promises to His people. God's covenant could be summarized by these words, "I am your God. You are my people." God alone established and preserves His relationship with people. God demonstrates His undeserved love toward believers in His covenant.

   Gen. 9:8–13—The world will no longer endure a universal flood. God places His rainbow in the sky as a sign of it.

   Gen. 12:1–3—God promises land, descendants, and blessing to Abraham. The blessing will be God's Son, Jesus Christ who will come to save the world.

2. God demonstrates His love in that He promises to place faith in our hearts and forgive and remember no more our sin.

3. Results of living under God's new covenant are as follows,

   Heb. 10:23—We can hold to the hope we profess; Christ paid the penalty and God has forgiven our sins.

   Heb. 10:24—Believers can urge others to love and to do good works.

   Heb. 10:25—We can encourage one another amid the trials of life.

   Heb. 10:35—We can be confident in the face of the dark and dreary moments of life.

   Heb. 10:39—We can believe, not doubt and fear, for God has saved us.

4. The results of living apart from the new covenant are as follows:

   Heb. 10:26—The person who willingly keeps on sinning has rejected the only sacrifice for forgiveness. By God's grace, however, such a person may be reinstated as a child of God when he or she repents.

Heb. 10:27—One who willingly keeps on sinning can expect only judgment.

Heb. 10:29—One who willingly keeps on sinning will be severely judged because that person has trampled on the Lord and insulted the Spirit.

Heb. 10:31—One who willingly keeps on sinning will fall into the hands of the living God for judgment.

5. The wonderful, life-saving Good News that Christ gives us in His Holy Meal is "My body given for you" and "My blood poured out for you." This meal is a proclamation of Christ's death on the cross where the penalty for our sins was paid. This is the best meal ever provided to people because it offers forgiveness of sins to all who believe.
6. Participants should have underlined: *forgiveness of sins, life, and salvation.*

Have participants repeat in unison Luther's explanation of the benefits of the best meal you can ever have.

Connect

Have a volunteer read the opening paragraph. Then invite participants to discuss in small groups the vignettes that follow. Allow groups to share with the entire class. Answers may vary.
1. God offered in His Supper the forgiveness of sins and the assurance of her salvation.
2. Sue and Jeff have received the continued assurance of their salvation, the forgiveness of sins committed against God and each other, and strength to lead a Christian life.
3. Andy received the forgiveness of sins and the renewed strength to lead a life worthy of his calling as a believer.

Have a volunteer read the final paragraph.

Vision

During This Week

Discuss these activities with the participants. Urge them to complete at least one during the week.

Closing Worship
Speak responsively the litany.

Scripture Lessons for Good Friday
Assign the appointed lessons for Good Friday.

Session 8

Good Friday

Isaiah 52:13–53:12 [Hosea 6:1–6]; Hebrews 4:14–16; 5:7–9;
John 18:1–19:42 [John 19:17–30]

Focus

Theme: *The Worst Suffering, the Best Result*

Law/Gospel Focus

Read aloud the Law/Gospel statement. Have participants underline once the Law statement in the first sentence and circle the Gospel statement in the second sentence.

Objectives

Read aloud or have a volunteer read the objectives aloud.

Opening Worship

Pray together the litany.

Introduction

Read aloud the vignette. Discuss the questions that follow either with the entire class or in small groups.
1. Responses will vary.
2. The suffering Jose experienced never affected the result of the tests. Regardless of the results of the tests, Jose's self-inflicted suffering could only bring him greater suffering.
3. The innocent, guiltless Son of God suffered for our sins and iniquities. Because of His obedience, even unto death, God declares us righteous through faith. This, for us, is the best kind of result.

Inform

If the participants have not read the lessons before class, it may be necessary to read the lessons aloud at this time. A brief summary of the lessons is provided in the study guide to help focus attention on the important messages of the texts.

The Old Testament lesson, Is. 52:13–53:12, speaks of God's suffering servant, Jesus Christ. The result of His suffering is the salvation of the world. He took upon Himself all the punishment deserved for our sin. We are to blame for the pain and suffering innocent Jesus willingly bore on the cross on our behalf.

The alternate Old Testament lesson, Hosea 6:1–6, calls all people to return to the Lord and to acknowledge Him. The Lord restores and gives us new life. He changes our hearts and our desires to live in faith.

The Epistle lesson, Heb. 4:14–16; 5;7–9, shows Christ in the heavenly sanctuary, who as a result of His death and resurrection, serves as our High Priest. He guarantees believers access to God because of His atonement for the sins of all people.

The Gospel lesson, John 18:1–19:42 [John 19:17–30], traces the day before the death of Jesus. The challenge is to not only see the historical injustices of that day, but to relate personally to the spiritual injustice of Christ being subjected to the penalty that was ours.

Have the participants work individually or in small groups to discuss the questions that follow the summaries.

1. The tragedy of the suffering servant is that He is totally innocent.
2. Jesus poured out His life blood for us on the cross. He who was innocent was numbered with the guilty.
3. Hosea talks about the Lord restoring us on the third day which enables us to live in the presence of God. He has removed our sins, the barrier to our relationship with Him.
4. Jesus has gone into heaven and He has sympathy with our plight on earth. He has experienced the same temptations that we experience. Yet, He never sinned.
5. In confidence we can approach the Almighty God and know that Jesus intercedes for us and understands us. We receive from our Lord the mercy and grace we need.
6. An innocent Jesus pleaded with God and submitted to His will by suffering and dying on the cross. The great result we received from His suffering was forgiveness of sins and eternal life.

7. John 18:4–9—Jesus knew all that was going to happen to Him and allowed Himself to be arrested.
   John 18:10–11—Jesus recognized that He must drink the cup of suffering the Father had given to Him.
   John 18:27; John 13:38—Jesus warned Peter that he would betray Him during the time of suffering.
   John 18:36—The kingdom of Jesus is not a worldly kingdom.
   John 19:11—Jesus says that the power over Him does not reside on earth but is greater than what is found on earth.
8. Through His suffering Jesus accomplished all that God set out for Him to do in order to give us the best result—salvation.

Connect

Ask a volunteer to read aloud the opening paragraph. Then discuss with the class the questions that follow.
1. Jesus was completely innocent of the crimes for which He was condemned. He, like Tom, willingly gave His life to save the life of the little girl.
2. Because of our sin, Jesus was stricken by God, smitten by Him, afflicted, pierced for our transgressions, and crushed for our iniquities.
3. Accept a variety of answers from participants. An innocent person does not deserve punishment.
4. We receive the best result because of Jesus' suffering. This is *good news* for us.

Vision

During This Week

Discuss these activities with the participants. Urge them to complete at least one of the activities during the week.

Closing Worship

Sing or pray together "The Agnus Dei."

Scripture Lessons for Next Sunday

Assign the appointed lessons for The Resurrection of Our Lord.

Session 9

The Resurrection of Our Lord

Exodus 15:1–11; 1 Corinthians 15:1–11; Luke 24:1–11

Focus

Theme: *He Won the Victory and So Did We*

Law/Gospel Focus

Read aloud the Law/Gospel focus. Help participants identify the Law and the Gospel. Have them underline the Law application once and circle the Gospel application. The Law application is found in the first sentence and the Gospel application in the second sentence.

Objectives

Choose a volunteer to read the objectives.

Opening Worship

Pray together the responsive verses.

Introduction

Read the opening and discuss with the entire class the question which ends the paragraph. Answers will vary.

Have a volunteer read each of the paragraphs that follow and discuss the questions that follow either with the entire class or in smaller groups.
1. Answers will vary.
2. Answers will vary. Point out that the resurrected Lord provides victory over sin, death, and the power of Satan in our lives.

Have a volunteer read the closing paragraph.

Inform

If participants have not read the lessons prior to class, it may be necessary to read the lessons aloud at this time. The study guide provides a brief summary of the lessons to help focus the participants' attention on the important messages found in each.

The first lesson, Ex. 15:1–11, is the song of Moses celebrating the victorious redemption God provided on the shores of the Red Sea. Pharaoh, who sarcastically asked "Who is God?" was completely and totally annihilated, dispossessed, and rooted out by God. Only a breath from God and the victory was won. Note also the activity of God's people who witnessed this wonderful deed. The Lord is their strength, their song, and their salvation.

In the Epistle lesson, 1 Cor. 15:1–11, Paul writes of the historic certainty of the Lord's victorious resurrection in response to Corinthian doubters. Paul's preaching the victory of Christ over the grave is linked to the faith which is believed.

The Gospel lesson, Luke 24:1–11, is the victorious resurrection story. The resurrection placed all the teachings of Jesus in a new perspective as the followers began to experience the risen and victorious Lord Jesus.

1. Answers will include the following—the Lord is highly exalted (Ex. 15:1); the Lord is my strength, my song, my salvation, my God (Ex. 15:2); the Lord is a warrior (Ex. 15:3); the Lord's right hand is majestic in power (Ex. 15:6).
2. The people sang songs of praise.
3. By the grace of God, Jesus Christ died and rose again in order to redeem us from our sin. We receive His gift of redemption through faith, not on the basis of our works.
4. Paul compares himself to the other apostles as one who was lifted out of his role as persecutor into the office of apostle.
5. The women were prepared to deal with the death of Jesus. They were going to complete the funeral customs. Certainly they must have been filled with grief over what had happened three days earlier. When they found Jesus had risen, the women went to tell the disciples. They must have been filled with amazement and excitement. When the disciples refused to believe their account at the tomb, the women might have been disappointed and frustrated.

Connect

1. Participants need not share their personal selections. However, allow participants to discuss these and additional ways to celebrate.
2. Responses might include serving as a Christian model of living, demonstrating concern, and being open to further opportunities to witness to the risen Christ. Remind participants that the Holy Spirit works through our faithful witness of the Word to create and strengthen that faith.
3. 1 Peter 2:24—He bore our sins so that we might die to sin and live in righteousness; 2 Tim. 1:10—He has destroyed death and brought us eternal life; 1 Cor. 15:55–57—Through the resurrection we are assured that life conquered death and has given us that victory through faith; 1 John 3:8—The work of the devil has been destroyed by Christ.
4. "A Mighty Fortress" (*LW* 297) shows that all material things we have are blessings from God. Yet, the greatest enduring blessing of all is the victorious faith that is ours as a free gift, given to us in our Baptism (see also Rom. 6:1–4). This faith sustains us throughout our lifetime, whether we are living in valleys of disaster or on mountaintops of joy.

Vision

During This Week

Suggest that participants complete one or more of the suggested activities.

As an alternative, read the activities and then have learners select the one they consider most important for them to accomplish. Discuss in pairs how they will complete the activity during the coming week.

Closing Worship

Sing or pray together the Easter hymn "Christ Jesus Lay in Death's Strong Bands" (*LW* 123) and/or read responsively the Easter Versicles.

Scripture Lessons for Next Sunday

Assign the appointed lessons for the Second Sunday of Easter.

Session 10

Second Sunday of Easter

Acts 5:12, 17–32; Revelation 1:4–18; John 20:19–31

Focus

Theme: *Surprise, Surprise, Surprise*

Law/Gospel Focus
Read aloud the Law/Gospel focus.

Objectives
Have a volunteer read aloud the objectives.

Opening Worship
Pray together the responsive reading from Ps. 105:1–4, 8.

Introduction

Read or have a volunteer read aloud the opening paragraph. Discuss the question that follows with the entire class.
1. You may want to begin the discussion by sharing a personal surprise. Answers will vary.
   Have a volunteer read aloud the next paragraph. Discuss the questions that follow with the entire class.
2. While answers will vary, help the participants to acknowledge such spiritual surprises as forgiveness of sins, eternal life, comfort and strength in trouble, and support to overcome sinful living provided by the Holy Spirit working through the Word and through the sacraments.

Inform

Hopefully, participants have read the lessons before class. However, if they have not, you may need to read all of the lessons aloud. A summary of the lessons is provided in the study guide to help focus the participants' attention.

The first lesson, Acts 5:12, 17–32, explodes surprise for the religious leaders and the disciples. Not only did God perform miracles through the apostles, He also performs miracles on the disciples behalf by releasing them from prison. The Jewish leaders are surprised that the Gospel cannot be bound but continues to be preached. He who rose from the grave is also able to perform surprising deeds on behalf of His disciples.

In the second lesson, Rev. 1:4–18, the apostle John, inspired by the Holy Spirit, peeks into heaven. He sees His Lord who is, who was, and who is to come—the past, present, and future—as the almighty ruler of kings. A description is given of Jesus in heaven. Jesus reassures John, who is gripped by fear, of His love because He is the first and last, the living One from the dead.

The Gospel lesson, John 20:19–31, provides more surprises. Jesus' appearance frightens the disciples. Amidst their fear He offers peace. Jesus gives them the power to forgive and retain sins. Thomas demands physical proof of the risen Lord and receives it the next week. What a surprise for him! The Lord leaves us with the comfort that He will bless those who, through faith, see Him.

1. God's surprises include the disciples' performance of miracles, their release from jail by God, and their continued proclamation of the Gospel. In spite of Jesus' surprising intervention, the Jewish leaders did not recognize His power.
2. He made the statement to the religious leaders who were supposed to represent God. What a surprise that they did not know Jesus and that Peter, a fisherman, did.
3. Alpha and Omega are the first and last letters of the Greek alphabet. Jesus is the first and last. This is the title used by God Himself in Is. 44:6 and Is. 48:12.
4. He saw Jesus in heaven dressed in a robe; with a golden sash; His head and hair were white; His eyes were blazing; His feet were like bronze glowing; His voice like rushing waters; He held seven stars; out of His mouth came a double-edged sword; and His face was like sun shining.

   John experienced first-hand the risen and exalted Lord Jesus Christ.
5. He was not with the disciples when Jesus appeared, and demanded physical proof of the resurrection. A week later, the risen Christ

confronted Thomas. He touched the hands and the side of Jesus and came to believe.
6. Those who have not seen, yet believe are given His Word and His sacraments as testimonies to the truth of His resurrection. By God's surprising intervention in people's lives, through Word and through sacrament, the Holy Spirit creates and strengthens saving faith in Jesus.
7. First lesson—The fear of the disciples who are arrested turns to peace as God opens the jail—a surprising intervention.

    Second lesson—John is frightened as he glimpses into heaven and sees the living Christ. Fear melts into peace as the living Lord intervenes, assuring him not to be afraid.

    Gospel lesson—The disciples are locked behind closed doors out of fear. Jesus' surprising appearance provides them peace.

Connect

Read the opening paragraph and discuss the questions either with the entire class or in small groups.
1. Through the means of grace—Word and sacraments—God does surprising works in our lives. Answers include,
    Eph. 2:8–9—God saves us by His grace.
    Titus 3:5—God saved us by the washing of regeneration in Baptism.
    Rom. 15:13—God gives believers joy, peace, and hope.
    Matt. 26:27–28—God gives us His Son's body and blood for the forgiveness of sins.
    2 Cor. 5:17—God makes us a new creation.
2. Answers will vary.
3. Answers will vary. Lead participants to acknowledge that our risen Lord and Savior, who is the first and the last, is with us in our fears, surprising us with His peace.
4. God has justified us by faith which gives us peace in our relationship with Him and assures us that He is with us in both good times and bad.

Vision

During This Week

Urge participants to complete one or more of the suggested activities during the coming week.

Closing Worship

Sing or pray together "O Sons and Daughters of the King" (*LW* 130).

Scripture Lessons for Next Sunday

Assign the appointed lessons for the Third Sunday of Easter.

Session 11

Third Sunday of Easter

Acts 9:1–20; Revelation 5:11–14; John 21:1–14

Focus

Theme: *Once Was Blind but Now I See*

Law/Gospel Focus

Have the participants cover up the Law/Gospel Focus. Read aloud only the first sentence. Ask, "Is this Law or Gospel?" When they determine this is Law, have them formulate a sentence of Gospel. Then compare the second sentence with their Gospel statement.

Objectives

Read the objectives in unison with the participants.

Opening Worship

Speak together responsively the prayer and then sing or speak "This is the feast" from *LW* pp. 161–63.

Introduction

Ask, "Where have you heard the theme for today?" Help them by saying, "It is in a hymn." When they have identified the hymn as "Amazing Grace," (*LW* 509) ask for a volunteer to read the paragraph.

Discuss the questions that follow either with the entire class or in small groups.
1. Sin and disobedience cause us to be hostile toward and blind to God.
2. Sin manifests itself in actions contrary to God's will.
3. The risen Lord has given us forgiveness and redemption; He has not counted our sins against us. He gives all this to us when we came to faith.

Inform

If the participants have not read the lessons prior to the class session, it may be necessary to read the lessons aloud. A summary of the lessons is provided in the study guide to help focus attention on their important messages.

The first lesson, Acts 9:1–20, focuses our attention on the eye-opening experience of a man named Saul. By the direct intervention of the Lord in his life, everything changes for him. He becomes Paul, the apostle to the Gentiles. Ananias serves at the command of the Lord in the most difficult of situations, for he thinks he faces certain capture, persecution, and/or death at the hands of the notorious persecutor of Christians, Saul. Paul is healed of both his physical blindness and spiritual blindness by God's miraculous intervention.

The second lesson, Rev. 5:11–14, provides a glimpse of worship in heaven. The angels, in a loud voice, sing about the victory that the Lamb of God has accomplished and what He has received as a result. Every creature in all of creation worships Christ, the Lamb who sits upon the throne, and gives Him the appropriate recognition He deserves. Refer to "This is the Feast" spoken or sung during the Opening Worship.

The Gospel reading, John 21:1–14, shows that Peter, the former fisherman, could not just sit around and wait. He and six others return to fish in the Sea of Galilee and catch nothing. The unrecognized Jesus tells them to try again. When their nets are filled, they immediately recognize Him. Peter rushes to shore to be with the Lord, and the others follow. Together the disciples and Jesus share a breakfast that Jesus had prepared.

Have the participants work individually or in small groups to discuss the questions that follow the summaries.

1. God worked an eye-opening miracle of conversion in the life of Saul so that he became Paul, the missionary to the Gentiles. Remind participants that they too experienced the miracle of conversion in their Baptism, or whenever they first came to the faith.
2. Ananias may have believed that he faced certain death at the hands of the Christian "head-hunter" Saul.
3. The key words include power—Jesus controls everything; wealth—Jesus owns everything; wisdom—Jesus knows everything; strength—Jesus overcomes everything; honor—Jesus is above everything; glory—Jesus is beyond everything; praise—Jesus is

greater than everything; and honor—Jesus is King of kings and Lord of lords.
4. The disciple whom Jesus loved, considered by many to be John, identified the man as Jesus.
5. They heard His voice and they saw Him but did not recognize Him. Jesus told them to fish on the side of the boat. After the large catch of fish the disciples recognized Him as their Lord and Savior. Jesus had risen from the dead and was alive again.

Connect

Ask a volunteer to read the story aloud. Ask them to work in small groups to complete the questions. Answers will vary. Urge participants to give specific examples. If time permits, have small groups report the substance of their discussion to the entire class.

Remind participants that God provides us with the faith strengthening means—His Word and His sacraments—through which the Holy Spirit works to keep our eyes fixed on Jesus.

Vision

During This Week

Carefully read and discuss each activity and then urge participants to complete one or both of them during the coming week.

Closing Worship

Pray the responsive reading.

Scripture Lessons for Next Sunday

Assign the appointed lessons for the Fourth Sunday of Easter.

Session 12

Fourth Sunday of Easter

Acts 13:15–16a, 26–33; Revelation 7:9–17; John 10:22–30

> ## Focus
>
> **Theme:** *The Lamb Is the Shepherd*
>
> **Law/Gospel Focus**
>
> Read aloud the Law/Gospel focus. Point out the Law application in the first sentence and the Gospel application in the second sentence.
>
> **Objectives**
>
> Ask participants to rephrase each objective in their own words.
>
> **Opening Worship**
>
> Pray together the responsive verses from John 10:14 and Ps. 23.

Introduction

Ask the participants to close their eyes for a moment and think about an image of Jesus they remember most. Ask participants to open their eyes and share the picture. List participants' responses on a board or on a sheet of newsprint.

After reading and discussing the opening paragraph, discuss the activities of the Good Shepherd that the participants have checked. Ask the entire group to help further define what is meant by each.

You may first want to share a life illustration to help the group open up.

Have a volunteer read the closing sentence. Then ask the whole group to respond with a personal answer to the question. Accept all answers.

Inform

It is hoped that participants have carefully read the lessons before class. However, you may need to read all of the lessons aloud. A summary of the lessons is provided in the study guide to help focus the participants' attention on important messages of the texts.

In the first lesson, Acts 13:15–16a, 26–33, Paul at the invitation of the leaders of the synagogue in Pisidian Antioch proclaims the message of salvation. He talks about the fulfillments of prophecy and of the trial and execution of the innocent Jesus. God, he said, raised Jesus from the dead and many people saw the Risen Lord.

In the second lesson, Rev. 7:9–17, John saw the Lamb upon the throne to whom belongs praise, glory, wisdom, thanks, honor, power, and strength. Those who have endured tribulation serve the Lamb who is the Shepherd. They never hunger or endure heat but are led by the Shepherd to springs of living water. God will wipe away their tears.

In the Gospel reading, John 10:22–30, Jesus answers the Jews and tells them He is the Christ and His miracles testify to it. His sheep hear the message of their Shepherd and follow Him. They receive eternal life and are secure in Him.

1. Isaiah 53:4–5—The Lamb took upon Himself our infirmities, carried our sorrows, was stricken by God, smitten and afflicted by Him, pierced for our transgressions, crushed for our iniquity, and was punished to give us peace. By His wounds we are healed.

   John 10:17–18—The Lamb laid down His life for us.

   John 1:29—The Lamb took away the sin of the world.

   1 John 1:7—The Lamb gives believers light, fellowship with one another, and purifies us from all sin.

   1 John 2:2—The Lamb is the atoning sacrifice for our sins and for the sins of the world.

2. Answers will vary. Highlight the everlasting nature of worshiping the Almighty God and His Son, the Lamb.

3. Those in heaven are described as standing before the throne, serving the Lamb, and being sheltered by God. There is no hunger or thirst, nor will the sun or scorching heat harm them. The Lamb is their Shepherd who leads them to springs of living water and wipes away their tears.

4. The Lamb and the Shepherd are one and the same—the Lord Jesus. He sits upon the throne and leads His people to living water and will comfort His sheep.

5. Believers follow Jesus and He gives them eternal life and security.

He promises that no one will snatch His sheep from Him and the Father.
6. The Shepherd knows His sheep, gives them eternal life, will never let His sheep perish, and will not let anyone snatch them away from Him.

The Sheep listen to the Shepherd's voice and follow it.

Connect

Have a volunteer read the opening paragraphs. Discuss the questions that follow with the entire class or in small groups.
1. Accept all answers. Explain that the Lord keeps us from harm and constantly watches over us.
2. Accept all answers. The Lord protects and strengthens us against Satan.
3. John 6:35—Jesus is the Bread of Life who strengthens us in the saving faith.
   John 7:37—Jesus quenches our desires, helping us to find rest in Him.
   John 9:5—Jesus is the light of the world.
   John 11:25–26—Jesus is the resurrection and the life.
   John 15:5—Jesus is the true vine. He keeps us connected to Him and in fellowship with one another.
4. Allow participants to check the responses that apply to them. Then ask for volunteers to explain why they checked various items.

Vision

During This Week

Ask a different volunteer to read each activity. Have participants circle the one which they will most likely accomplish in the coming week.

Closing Worship

Sing or pray together "At the Lamb's High Feast We Sing" (*LW* 126).

Scripture Lessons for Next Sunday

Assign the appointed lessons for the Fifth Sunday of Easter.

Session 13

Fifth Sunday of Easter

Acts 13:44–52; Revelation 21:1–5; John 13:31–35

> ## Focus
>
> **Theme:** *What's New about Love?*
>
> ### Law/Gospel Focus
> Read aloud the Law/Gospel focus. Help participants identify the Law and the Gospel.
>
> ### Objectives
> Read aloud and briefly discuss the objectives.
>
> ### Opening Worship
> Pray together the responsive reading from Ps. 145:1–2, 8.

Introduction

Show the participants a large red heart and ask them, "What does this represent?" Discuss the meaning of the symbol in the culture. After the discussion announce the theme as love and ask a volunteer to read the introductory paragraph.

1. Love is characterized in three examples:
   a. friendship and brotherly love,
   b. erotic love, and
   c. sacrificial love.

   Have a volunteer read the next paragraph.

2. Positive motives for love might include witnessing faith in Jesus, obeying the Lord, and responding to what God has accomplished for me. Negative motives for love might include receiving something in return, obtaining a favor, and accomplishing my goals.

Inform

It is hoped that participants have carefully read the lessons before class. However, you may need to read all of the lessons aloud. A summary of the lessons is provided in the study guide to help focus the participants' attention.

In the first lesson, Acts 13:44–52, word had spread of Paul's message so that on the next Sabbath almost the whole city gathered to hear the Word of the Lord. The Gospel message was rejected by the Jews, so Paul turned to the Gentiles. The Word of the Lord grew throughout the region, but the Jews initiated steps to end Paul's ministry. As a result the apostle left.

In the second lesson, Rev. 21:1–5, John describes the new heaven and the new earth where God will wipe every tear and eliminate death, mourning, crying, and pain.

In the Gospel lesson, John 13:31–35, the exit of Judas sets the stage for a series of events that would ultimately lead to Jesus' crucifixion. In death our Lord would be glorified, fulfilling the Father's purposes. The new commandment of love is given. This love was modeled by Christ in His life and in His death. Such love would be a testimony to the world as people recognize that it is from God.

1. The Jews were jealous and talked abusively to Paul.
2. Paul was persecuted and the Gospel message was rejected. Paul shook the dust from his feet and left Pisidian Antioch to share the Good News with others.
3. Jesus promises a new heaven and earth where believers will live in eternal bliss with Him.
4. People are inclined toward evil from their youth, beginning with desire that bears sin and results in death.
5. 1 John 3:16—Jesus showed His love by laying down His life for us. Titus 2:14—Jesus gave Himself to redeem us and to purify for
    Himself a people that His is very own, eager to do what is good.
6. People will know that we are Jesus' disciples by our love for one another.
7. Ask the entire group to read silently 1 Cor. 13:4–7. Summaries of 1 Cor. 13:4–7 will include love is patient, kind, not envious, humble, not rude or self-seeking, not easily angered, rejoices in truth, protects, trusts, hopes, and perseveres.

Connect

Have a volunteer read aloud the opening paragraph. Have the participants work in small groups to discuss possible responses to each repentant sinner. Ask, "What is God's response to these repentant sinners?"

1. Although answers will vary, Jesus forgives completely all repentant sinners, no matter what sin they have committed.
2. A Christian is motivated by the love which Christ has shown by laying down His life for the forgiveness of sins. This motive differs from the selfish motive of an unbeliever who might be concerned with getting something in return for his/her love.
3. Read 1 Cor. 5:1–5. Emphasize verse 5. This verse points out the reason for demonstrating "tough love."

Vision

During This Week

Ask a volunteer to read the activity. Encourage the participants to complete the activity during the week.

Closing Worship

Sing or pray together stansas one and four of "Dear Christians, One and All" (*LW* 353).

Scripture Lessons for Next Sunday

Assign the appointed lessons for the Sixth Sunday of Easter.

Session 14

Sixth Sunday of Easter

Acts 14:8–18; Revelation 21:10–14, 22–23; John 14:23–29

Focus

Theme: *Departures and Arrivals*

Law/Gospel Focus

Read aloud the Law/Gospel focus. Point out the Law application in the first sentence and the Gospel application in the second sentence.

Objectives

Have a volunteer read aloud the objectives.

Opening Worship

Pray together the responsive reading from Ps. 66:1, 2, 8, 9, 20.

Introduction

Ask participants, "When you go to pick someone up at the airport, or to fly somewhere, what is the most important thing you need to know?" (Arrival and/or departure times.) Then say, "There are other departures and arrivals that are important." Have a volunteer read the introductory paragraphs.

Discuss the questions that follow with the entire class or in small groups.
1. Answers will vary. Have participants think of physical and emotional preparations that are needed.
2. Answers will vary.
3. Answers will vary.

Inform

It is hoped that participants have carefully read the lessons before class. However, you may need to read the lessons aloud. A summary of the lessons is provided in the study guide to help focus the participants' attention.

In the first lesson, Acts 14:8–18, a believing cripple is healed by Paul. Notice that the people did not look for a scientific reason, but rather immediately recognized it as a supernatural event. Mistakenly they identified Paul and Barnabas as Zeus and Hermes. Interestingly, they desire to offer sacrifices to them. Paul confesses the true God.

The Epistle lesson, Rev. 21:10–14, 22–23, is a description of the heavenly city. The Lord God Almighty and the Lamb are the temple. The glory of God is the light and the Lamb is identified as the lamp in heaven.

The Gospel reading, John 14:23–29, occurs in the upper room after the departure of Judas. This is part of a question and answer session with the disciples as our Lord is about to suffer and die. He provides His disciples (and us) with explanations for Christian living and relationships. He stresses love, obedience, and peace.

1. The people of Lystra desired to worship Paul and Barnabas rather than their Creator.
2. Paul and Barnabas tore their clothes as a sign of displeasure and confessed that they were merely the creatures of God and not God themselves.
3. The great, high wall symbolizes the entrance into heaven. Only those who believe in the risen Lord Jesus Christ will enter.

    The twelve gates, each having an angel, symbolize that the entrance into heaven is guarded to insure that only believers enter.

    The names of the twelve tribes of Israel symbolize the Old Testament believers who, in faith, looked forward to the coming Savior.

    The twelve foundations with twelve apostles' names symbolize the New Testament believers who, in faith, look back at the salvation accomplished by the risen Savior.
4. The Lord God Almighty and the Lamb are the temple. The glory of God is the source of light and the Lamb is the lamp.
5. Answers will be similar to the following:
    a. Those who love Christ will obey Him.

    b. Jesus is the object of our love.
    c. The object of obedience is the teaching of Christ.
    d. The Spirit (Counselor) will teach all things and remind us of what the Savior has said.
    e. Jesus gives us a peace unlike any other in the world.
    f. Jesus tells the disciples these things because He is going away and desires that they be informed about the true purpose of His departure.

Connect

Have a volunteer read the opening paragraph. Then share the section as a large group or in small groups.
1. Responses will vary. Share both physical and emotional responses to these life events.
2. Nah. 1:7 emphasizes that during trials and troubles the Lord continues to care for us.

    Rom. 8:38–39 says nothing can separate us from the love of God in Christ Jesus our Lord.

    Ps. 23 tells us that the Good Shepherd guides and cares for us in all life events.

Vision

During This Week

Have a different volunteer read each of the activities. Urge them to complete at least one during the coming week.

Closing Worship

Sing or pray together the hymn "Our Father, Who from Heaven Above" (*LW* 430).

Scripture Lessons for Ascension of Our Lord

Assign the appointed lessons for the Ascension of our Lord.

Session 15

The Ascension of Our Lord

Acts 1:1–11; Ephesians 1:16–23; Luke 24:44–53

Focus

Theme: *I Told You So!*

Law/Gospel Focus

Read aloud the Law/Gospel focus. Help participants identify the Law and the Gospel. Have them underline the Law application once and circle the Gospel application. The Law is found in the first sentence and the Gospel in the second.

Objectives

Read aloud the objectives.

Opening Worship

Pray together the responsive prayer.

Introduction

Ask a volunteer to read aloud the opening paragraph. Discuss the questions that follow in small groups. Allow groups to share with the entire class.

1. Answers will vary.
2. Encourage participants to think about and illustrate both the positive and negative aspects of the statement "I told you so!" Ask a volunteer in each of the groups to read the next paragraph. Then ask the groups to discuss the next question.
3. God provides information about our lives in the Bible. In Scripture, God talks to us about our sin and about our Savior. If time permits, read 2 Tim. 3:16–17.

Inform

If the participants have not read the lessons prior to the class session, read the lessons aloud. A summary of the lessons is provided in the study guide to help focus participants' attention on the important messages.

In the first lesson, Acts 1:1–11, Luke briefly introduces the book of Acts. During the forty days after His resurrection, Jesus demonstrated that He had risen and gave further explanation to His teachings. He promised to send His Spirit in order to empower the apostles to witness. As the followers watched He ascended into heaven. Two men dressed in white promised that Jesus would come again.

In the second lesson, Eph. 1:16–23, Paul gives thanks for the Ephesians. He asks the Lord to give them the Spirit of wisdom and revelation in order that they might better know the Lord, and to enlighten their hearts in order that they might know the hope to which God has called them. Christ is seated at the right hand of God in a position of authority, power, and dominion. God has given Him control over everything for the sake of His church.

In the Gospel reading, Luke 24:44–53, Jesus elaborates on how He has fulfilled the prophecies spoken about Him. He focuses the disciples' attention on the heart of apostolic preaching: Christ died and rose again, so repent and receive forgiveness for your sins. Jesus identifies His followers as witnesses. After He ascends into heaven, His disciples return to Jerusalem with great joy. Here they worship God continually in the temple.

Allow time for individuals to read and mark the true statements. All statements are true. Discuss each of the statements. Include the following details.

1. The convincing proof that Jesus gave to His disciples includes inviting them to see and touch His wounds, talking with them about His teaching, and His physical presence with them and many others.
2. The promised gift was the Holy Spirit.
3. First the apostles would receive power and then they would be witnesses. Notice the locations where they would witness: in Jerusalem, in all Judea and Samaria, and to the ends of the world. In a sense this forms the outline for the book of Acts.
4. Someday Jesus will return to the earth in the same visible, glorious way in which He had departed. We can anticipate with joy the

bodily return of Christ.
5. Paul prays that through the Spirit we may know the Lord Jesus Christ.
6. It is only as God enlightens us that we can truly know Him and the riches of His glory. The Spirit works this miracle in us through the Word and through the sacraments.
7. The very power of God raised Christ from the dead and placed Him at His right hand. This power is available to us through the Holy Spirit working through Word and through sacraments.
8. Christ's ultimate and complete victory has meant God appointed Him to be head of the Church and put everything under His control for the church's benefit.
9. The three main divisions of the Old Testament were the Law of Moses, the Prophets, and the Psalms. Jesus fulfills all the prophecies written about the Messiah.
10. Jesus shared with His disciples that He died and rose to earn salvation for all people. He promised that repentance and forgiveness will be preached in His name to all nations beginning in Jerusalem. Jesus identifies His followers as witnesses.
11. Jesus' disciples experienced joy at His departure because they came to know the reason for His ascension into heaven.
12. The focal point of their worship was God, and the place of worship was in His house, the temple.

Connect

Ask a volunteer to read the paragraph. Have small groups discuss the passages and then share their thoughts with the entire group.

Ps. 34:22—"The LORD redeems His servants; no one will be condemned who takes refuge in Him."

Ps. 118:8—"It is better to take refuge in the LORD than to trust in man."

Prov. 3:5—Trust the Lord, not your own understanding.

John 16:24—Jesus encourages us to complete our joy by asking Him for anything.

1 Thess. 5:18—God desires us to give thanks to God in all circumstances.

Read the next paragraph. God's "I told you so's" are promises for our lives. God will faithfully keep His promises to us because He told us He would.

Read the next paragraph. Allow time for participants to share their comforting "I told you so" passage from God's Word.

Vision

During This Week

Discuss the activities in class. Urge participants to complete one or more of the activities during the week.

Closing Worship

Split the class into two groups. Have the groups take turns reading lines from "Up through Endless Ranks of Angels" (*LW* 152).

Scripture Lessons for Next Sunday

Assign the appointed lessons for the Seventh Sunday of Easter.

Session 16

Seventh Sunday of Easter

Acts 16:6–10; Revelation 22:12–17, 20; John 17:20–26

Focus

Theme: *Behind Closed Doors*

Law/Gospel Focus

Read aloud the Law/Gospel focus. Help participants identify the Law and Gospel.

Objectives

Invite a volunteer to read aloud the objectives.

Opening Worship

Pray together the responsive reading from Rom. 6:9 and John 14:18.

Introduction

Ask a volunteer to read the opening paragraphs. Accept all answers to the questions. Answers will vary.

Inform

If the participants have not read the lessons prior to the class session, it may be necessary to read the lessons aloud. A summary of the lessons is provided in the study guide to help focus participants' attention on their important messages.

In the first lesson, Acts 16:6–10, the Holy Spirit closes a door for Paul's missionary work in Bithynia and Mysia only to open another for work in Macedonia.

In the second lesson, Rev. 22:12–17, our Lord calls Himself by various descriptive names. He is the Alpha and Omega, the First and the

Last, the Beginning and the End, the Root and the Offspring of David, and the bright Morning Star. He is coming soon to bring believers through the gates of the city while unbelievers will remain outside.

The Gospel lesson, John 17:20–26, is a portion of Jesus' High Priestly Prayer for the church. He asks the heavenly Father to keep unity among the believers in order that they might witness Christ to others. He prays that the believers may be with Him in heaven to see His glory which was given by the Father. He prays that the Father's love be present with His followers.

1. The Spirit kept Paul from preaching in Bithynia and Mysia. The door to preach in Macedonia was opened to Paul.
2. God provided the vision to open the door for Paul to preach the Gospel in Macedonia.
3. Those who have washed their robes have the right to the tree of life. They are believers who have received the gift of eternal life from God, through faith in Christ Jesus.
4. The door of heaven is closed to those who practice magic arts, the sexually immoral, the murderers, the idolaters, and everyone who loves and practices falsehood.
5. The Lord invites us to receive the free gift of salvation earned by the Lamb.
6. The Lord promises that when He returns He will gather His people. As believers we can look forward to the day when we will be with our Lord in heaven.
7. Jesus prays for unity among believers.
8. Jesus states that He and the Father are one.

Connect

Ask for a volunteer to read aloud the opening paragraph. Then discuss with the class the questions that follow.

1. Answers will vary
2. Accept all answers.
3. Ps. 23:2—God leads us to green pastures beside still waters, providing us with both temporal and spiritual blessings.
    Ps. 48:14—God guides us to the end.
    Ps. 73:24—God guides His faithful people with His counsel and takes us finally to eternity.

Is. 30:21—God directs our paths.
   John 10:11—Jesus, the Good Shepherd, laid down His life for you.
4. Answers will vary. The leader might suggest such examples as serving as a peacemaker between two people; working to resolve diverse doctrinal issues through the study of God's word; serving in a church office; or teaching.
5. For the believer, death is the door that leads to eternal life.
   a. Christ has won victory over death and has given us eternal life.
   b. God gives us victory through our Lord Jesus Christ.
   c. The Lord is with us and has accomplished our salvation.
   d. Those who labor for the Lord do not do so in vain.

Vision

During This Week

Review the activities in class and urge participants to complete them during the week.

Closing Worship

Sing or pray together "Christ Is the World's Redeemer" (*LW* 271).

Scripture Lessons for Next Sunday

Assign the appointed lessons for the festival of Pentecost.

Session 17

The Festival of Pentecost

Genesis 11:1–9; Acts 2:37–47; John 15:26–27; 16:4b–11

Focus

Theme: *Gathering to Scatter*

Law/Gospel Focus

Read aloud the Law/Gospel focus.

Objectives

Read aloud the objectives to the class.

Opening Worship

Pray together the litany based upon the hymn "Come, Holy Ghost, God and Lord" (*LW* 154).

Introduction

Ask, "What do you remember about the last Olympics?" Allow one or two to respond. Have a volunteer read the opening paragraphs. Then discuss the questions that follow, either in the entire class or in small groups.

1. God created our saving faith in Jesus when we received the Holy Spirit through Holy Baptism. We received the blessings of forgiveness of sins and eternal life.
2. God continues to strengthen our faith in Jesus as the Holy Spirit works through God's Word and the Lord's Supper.

Inform

It is hoped that participants have read carefully the lessons before class. However, you may need to read all of the lessons aloud. A summary of the lessons is provided in the study guide to help focus the participants' attention.

The Old Testament lesson, Gen. 11:1–9, is the story of the Tower of Babel and God's dealing with the selfish plans of the builders. God confuses their language and scatters them abroad. Some have viewed Pentecost, where people hear the Gospel in their own tongue, as a reversal of the confusion of tongues at Babel.

The second lesson, Acts 2:37–47, occurs after Peter has preached his Pentecost sermon. The result is the formation of the community of faith which engages in continued spiritual growth as the Holy Spirit works in their midst through the means of grace.

In the Gospel lesson, John 15:26–27; 16:4b–11, Jesus promises to send the Holy Spirit. The Spirit brings a testimony of Law and Gospel to hearers' hearts.

1. As a result of their sinful self-centeredness, they denied the power of God and attempted to bring glory to themselves rather then give glory to God. Therefore, the Lord scattered them across the world.
2. The Lord responded in three ways: He scattered the people of Babel across the world, He confused their language, and He stopped them from building.
3. The hearers asked Peter what they must do. Peter told them they must repent and be baptized and they would receive the Holy Spirit.
4. The community of believers devoted themselves to the apostles' teaching; joined in fellowship; broke bread; prayed; shared everything; met in the temple; ate together; and praised God. Note the two main Note the two main focuses of the liturgy alluded to here: Word (Apostles' teaching) and Sacraments (breaking of bread).
5. God scatters those whom He has gathered so that they might proclaim His love to all people. Directions to the scattered church include,
    Matthew 5:14–16—We, as the light of the world, point others to God as we let our light shine.
    Matthew 16:24—We deny ourselves, take up our crosses, and follow Jesus.
    Galatians 5:13—We serve one another in love.
    Galatians 5:22–23—We manifest the fruit of the Spirit in our Christian living.
    Ephesians 5:18–20—We avoid sin and, relying on the Spirit, speak and sing about God's goodness, thanking and praising God for everything in the name of our Lord Jesus.
6. The Lord sent His Spirit on the Day of Pentecost when the disci-

ples were together. He came with a sound like a mighty wind and the appearance of tongues of fire.
7. The Spirit works through the means of grace—the Word, Baptism, and the Lord's Supper—to "call, gather, enlighten, and sanctify" His people.

Connect

Ask a volunteer to read aloud the opening paragraph. Have participants work independently to apply each of the Scripture references to their lives. If time permits allow participants to share their responses in small groups or with the large group.
1. Although God is serious about sin and punishes those who resist His power, in Christ He provides the forgiveness of sins and eternal life to all repentant hearts.
2. Christians study God's word, share His love in fellowship with one another, celebrate the Lord's Supper, and pray.
3. Christians regularly worship the Lord.
4. Believers witness Christ through their words and actions.
5. Believers have received the gift of the Holy Spirit through whom they receive the power to witness Christ.

Ask a volunteer to read aloud the closing paragraph.

Vision

During This Week

Ask participants to select one or more of the activities to complete prior to the next session.

Closing Worship

Sing or pray together the Pentecost hymn "Come, Holy Ghost, God and Lord" (*LW* 154).

Scripture Lessons for Next Sunday

Assign the appointed lessons for Trinity Sunday.